Alfred's Basic Piano Library

Praise Hits
Complete Levels 2 & 3
For the Later Beginner

Arranged by Tom Gerou

Produced by
Alfred Music
P.O. Box 10003
Van Nuys, CA 91410-0003
alfred.com

Printed in USA.

ISBN-10: 1-4706-1958-X
ISBN-13: 978-1-4706-1958-9

Cover Photos
Meadow at morning: © Shutterstock.com / Galyna Andrushko • Deco sun: © Shutterstock.com / Mark Grenier

Foreword

This series answers the often expressed need for contemporary Christian music to be used as supplementary pieces for students. Soon after beginning piano study, students can play attractive versions of the best-known praise music of today.

This book is correlated page-by-page with Lesson Book, Complete Levels 2 & 3 of *Alfred's Basic Piano Library*; pieces should be assigned based on the instructions in the upper-right corner of each title page of *Praise Hits*. Since the melodies and rhythms of praise music do not always lend themselves to precise grading, you may find that these pieces are sometimes a little longer and more difficult than the corresponding pages in the Lesson Book. The teacher's judgment is the most important factor in deciding when to assign each arrangement.

When the books in the *Praise Hits* series are assigned in conjunction with the Lesson Books, these appealing pieces reinforce new concepts as they are introduced. In addition, the motivation the music provides could not be better. The emotional satisfaction that students receive from mastering each praise song increases their enthusiasm to begin the next one.

Contents

Use with Alfred's Basic Piano Library
Complete Lesson Book 2 & 3, after page 8.

Forever

Words and Music by Chris Tomlin
Arr. by Tom Gerou

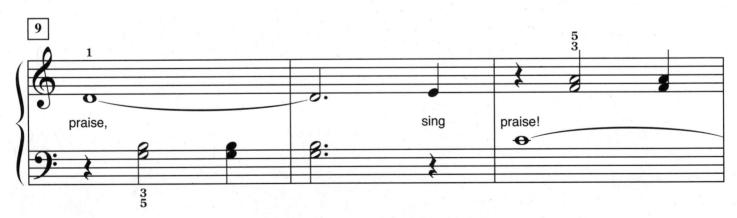

Use after pages 10–11.

Lord, I Lift Your Name On High

Words and Music by Rick Founds
Arr. by Tom Gerou

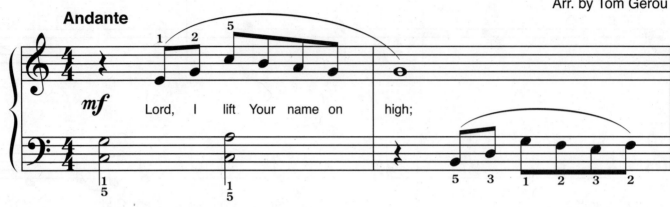

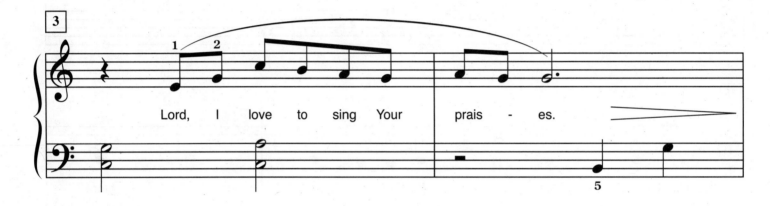

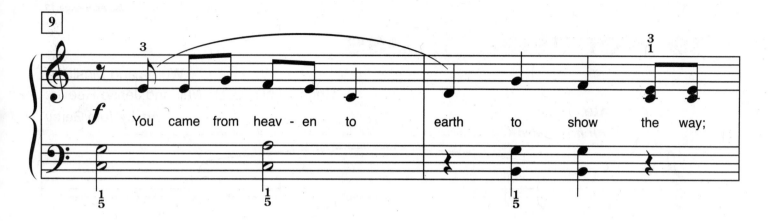

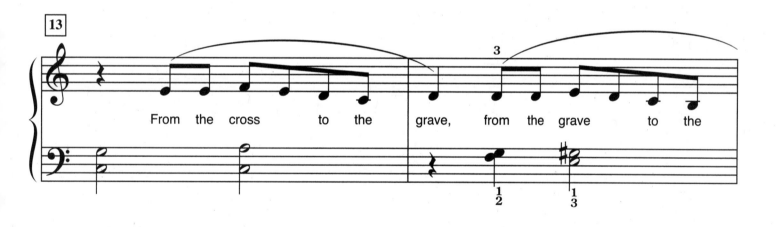

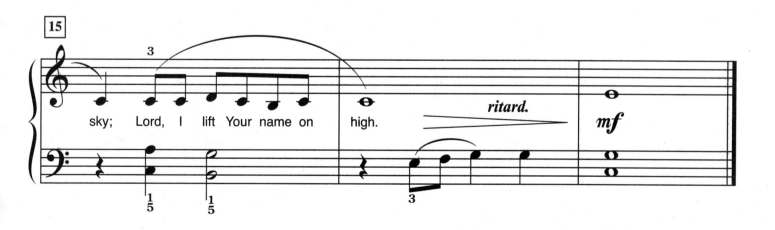

Use after page 13.

The Wonderful Cross

Words and Music by
Chris Tomlin, J. D. Walt and Jesse Reeves
Arr. by Tom Gerou

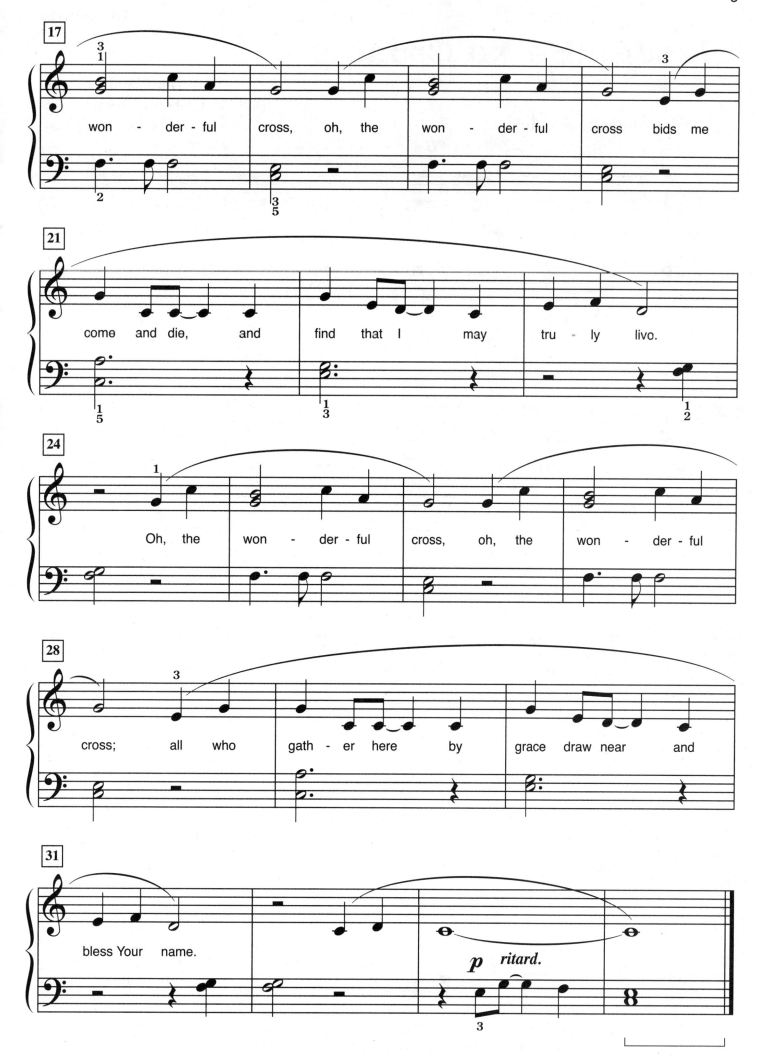

Blessed Be Your Name

Words and Music by
Beth Redman and Matt Redman

Arr. by Tom Gerou

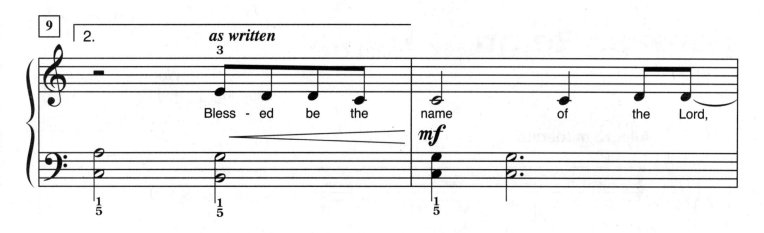

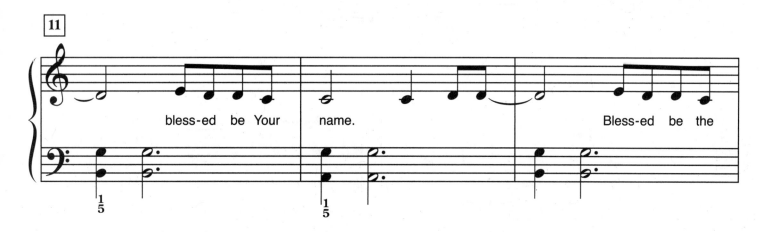

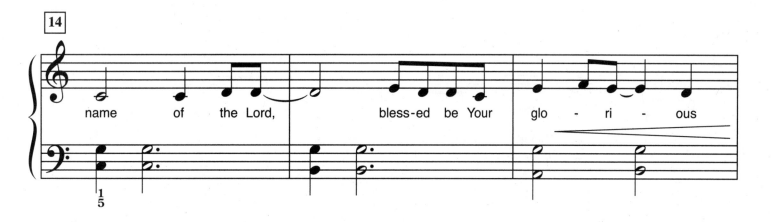

Use after page 19.

Forever Reign

Words and Music by
Jason Ingram and Reuben Morgan
Arr. by Tom Gerou

Allegro moderato

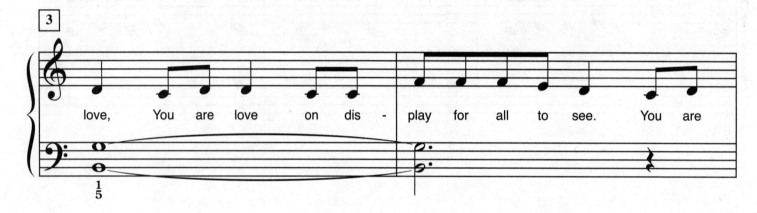

Use after page 22.

Holy Is the Lord

Words and Music by
Chris Tomlin and Louie Giglio
Arr. by Tom Gerou

Moderato

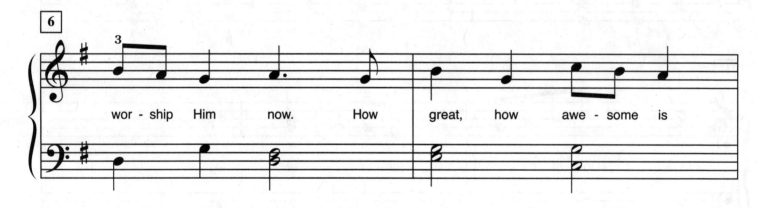

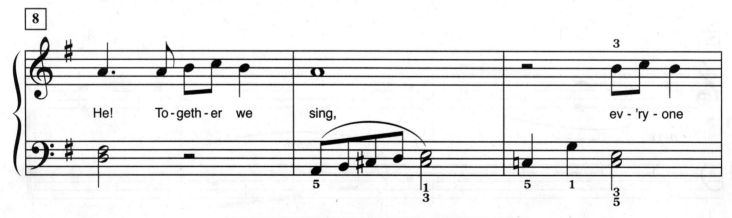

Use after page 25.

Hosanna
(Praise Is Rising)

Words and Music by
Brenton Brown and Paul Baloche

Arr. by Tom Gerou

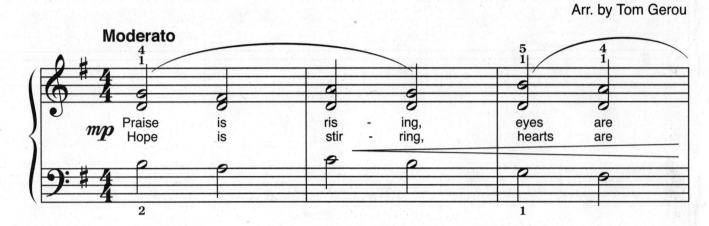

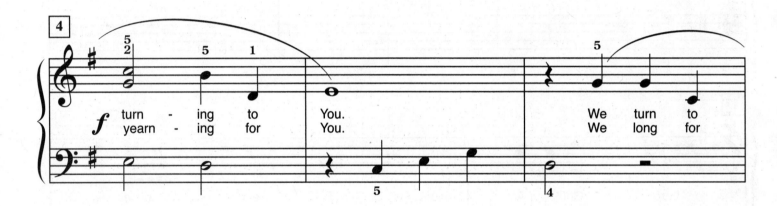

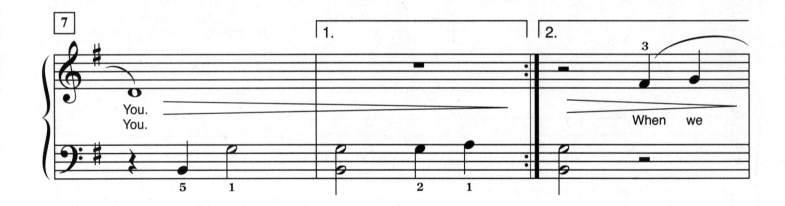

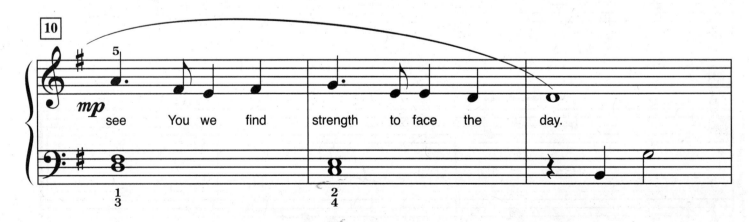

Use after pages 26–27.

Revelation Song

Words and Music by Jennie Lee Riddle
Arr. by Tom Gerou

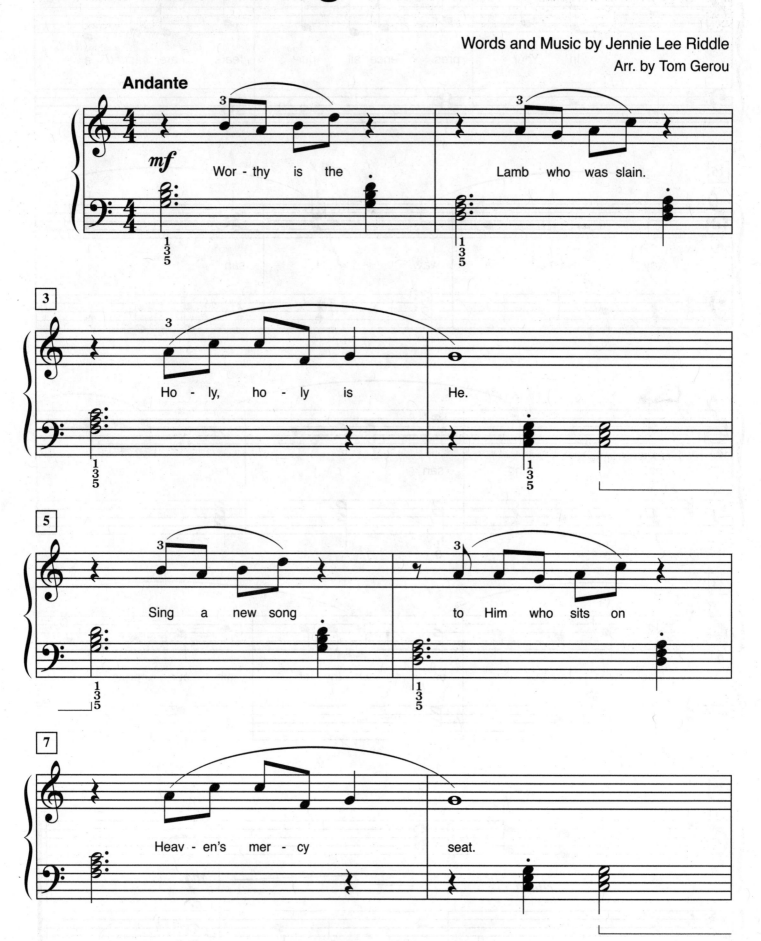

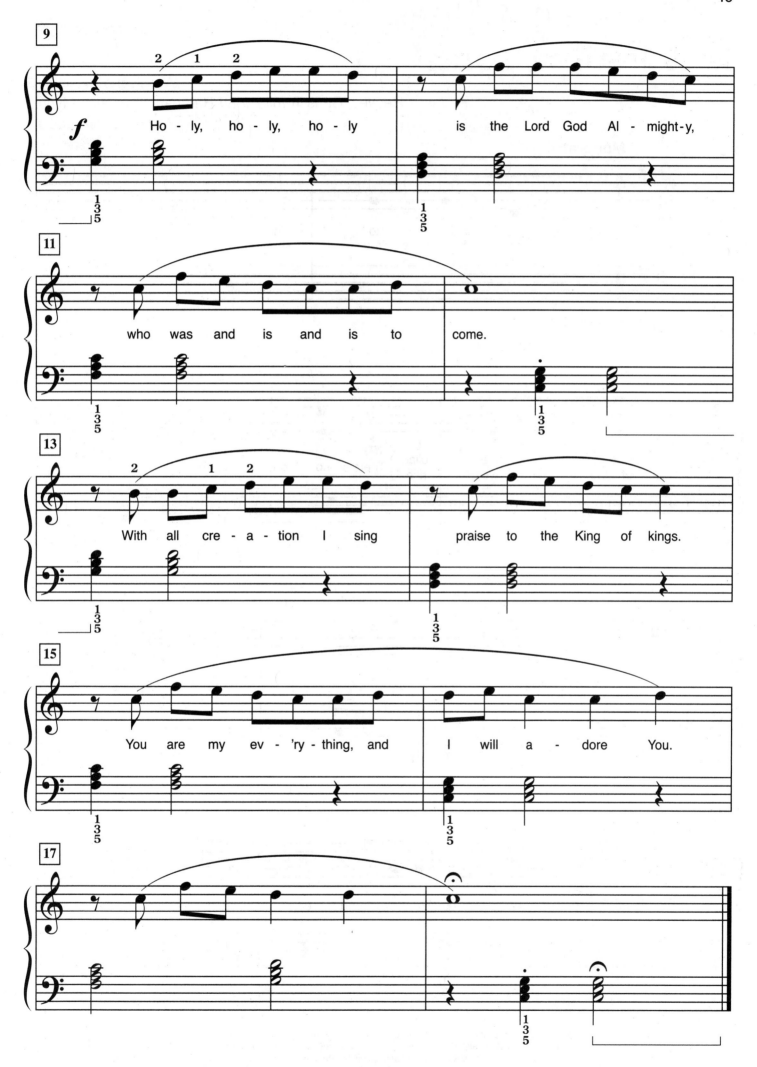

Use after page 32.

Our God

Words and Music by
Jesse Reeves, Chris Tomlin, Matt Redman and Jonas Myrin
Arr. by Tom Gerou

Use after page 38.

Here I Am to Worship
(Light of the World)

Words and Music by Tim Hughes
Arr. by Tom Gerou

Page 23

Use after pages 40–41.

Your Grace Is Enough

Words and Music by Matt Maher
Arr. by Tom Gerou

Great is Your faith - ful - ness, oh God.

You wres-tle with the sin - ner's heart.

You lead us by still wa - ters in - to mer - cy,

and noth - ing can keep us a - part.

Use after pages 42–43.

In Christ Alone
(My Hope Is Found)

Words and Music by
Stuart Townend and Keith Getty

Arr. by Tom Gerou

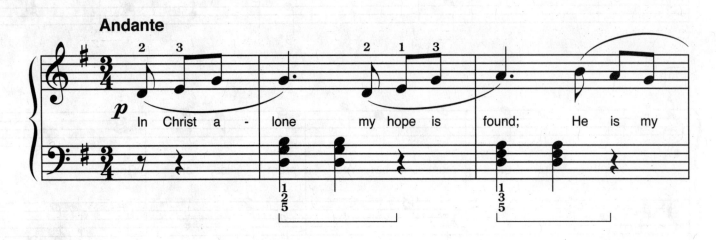

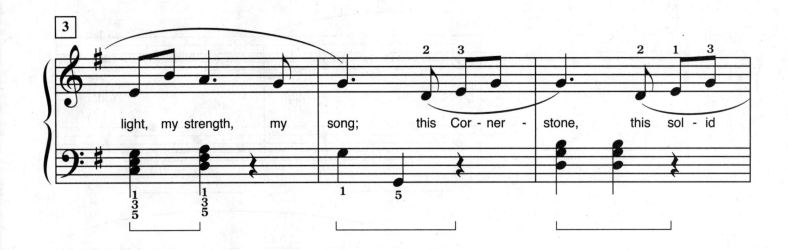

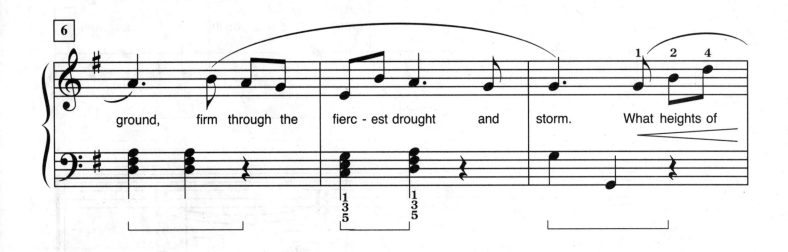

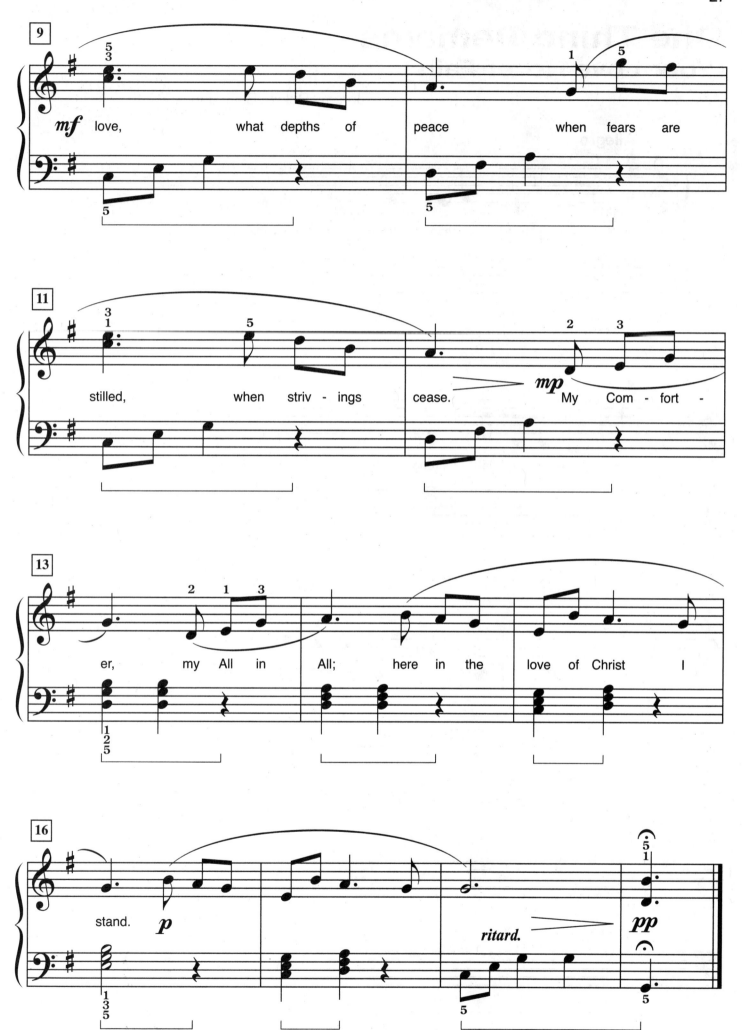

Use after pages 46–47.

One Thing Remains
(Your Love Never Fails)

Words and Music by
Jeremy Riddle, Brian Johnson and Christa Black
Arr. by Tom Gerou

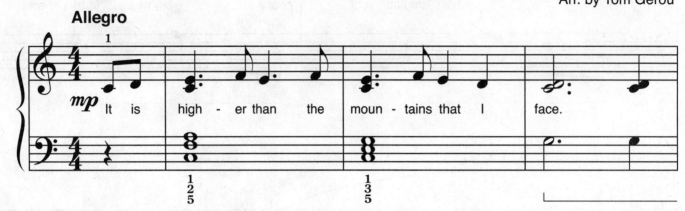

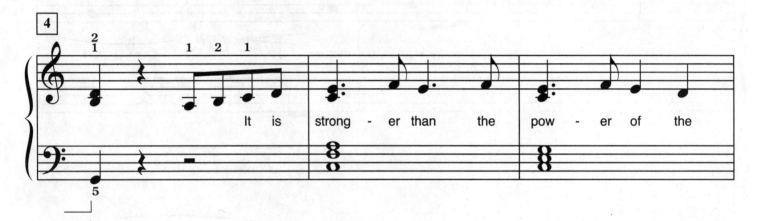

Use after pages 52–53.

10,000 Reasons
(Bless the Lord)

Words and Music by
Matt Redman and Jonas Myrin

Arr. by Tom Gerou

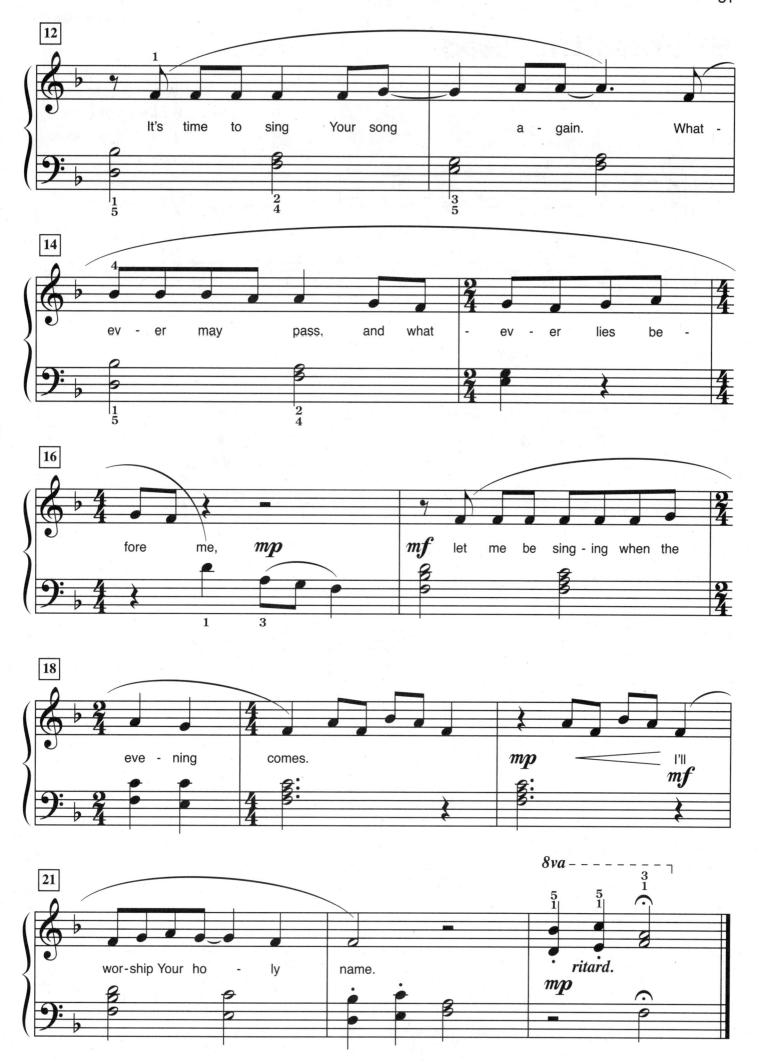

Use after page 56.

Everlasting God

Words and Music by
Brenton Brown and Ken Riley

Arr. by Tom Gerou

Allegro

mf Strength will rise as we wait up - on the Lord, we will wait

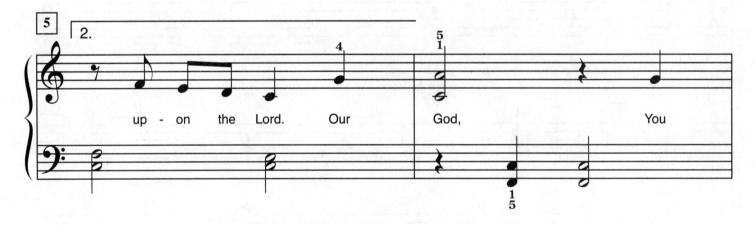

up - on the Lord, we will wait up - on the Lord.

1.

2. up - on the Lord. Our God, You

reign for - ev - er. Our Hope, our

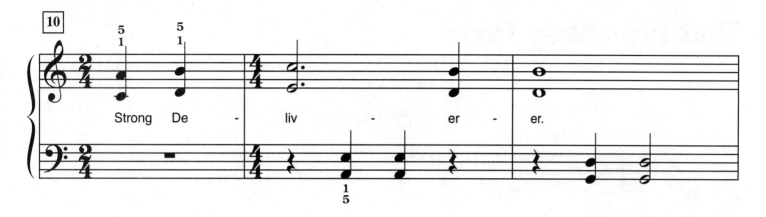

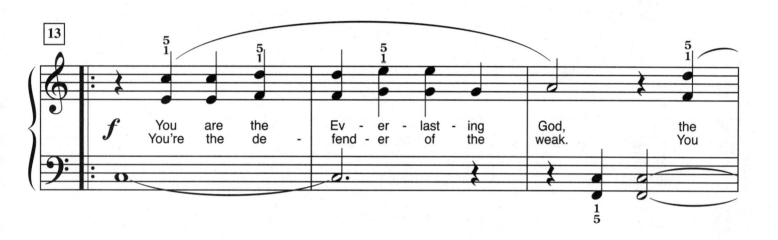

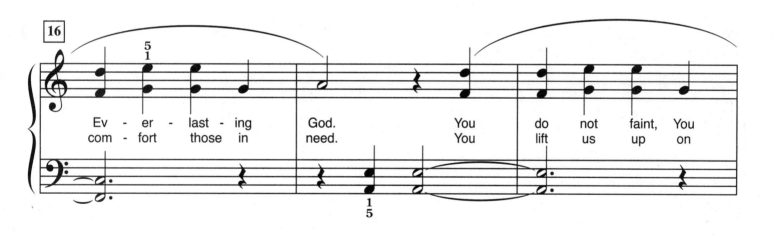

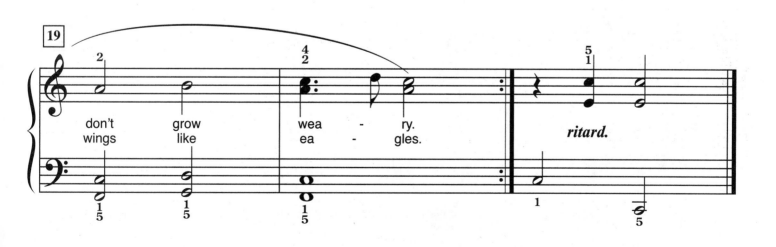

Use after pages 60–61.

Jesus Messiah

Words and Music by
Daniel Carson, Chris Tomlin, Ed Cash and Jesse Reeves

Arr. by Tom Gerou

Use after pages 64–65.

Hosanna

Words and Music by Brooke Ligertwood
Arr. by Tom Gerou

Use after page 66.

Mighty to Save

Words and Music by
Reuben Morgan and Ben Fielding
Arr. by Tom Gerou

Ev'ry-one needs com - pas - sion, a love that's nev - er

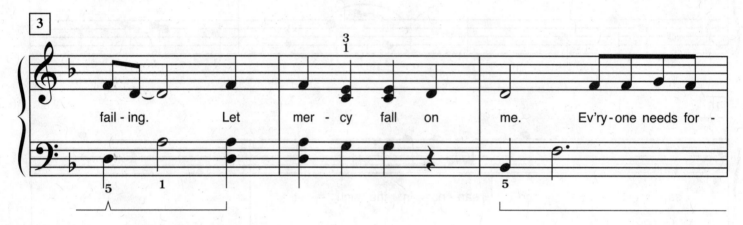

fail - ing. Let mer - cy fall on me. Ev'ry-one needs for -

give-ness, the kind-ness of a Sav - ior, the Hope of na - tions.

Use after pages 68–69.

From the Inside Out

Words and Music by Joel Houston
Arr. by Tom Gerou

A thou - sand times I've failed, still Your

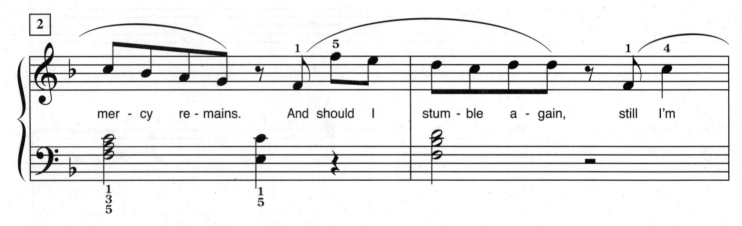

mer - cy re - mains. And should I stum - ble a - gain, still I'm

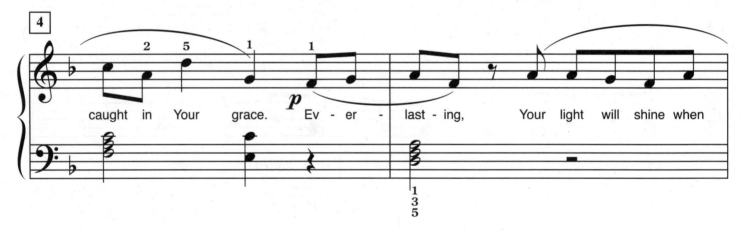

caught in Your grace. Ev - er - last - ing, Your light will shine when

all else fades. Nev - er - end - ing Your glo - ry goes be - yond all fame.

Use after pages 70–71.

Indescribable

Words and Music by
Jesse Reeves and Laura Story
Arr. by Tom Gerou

Moderato

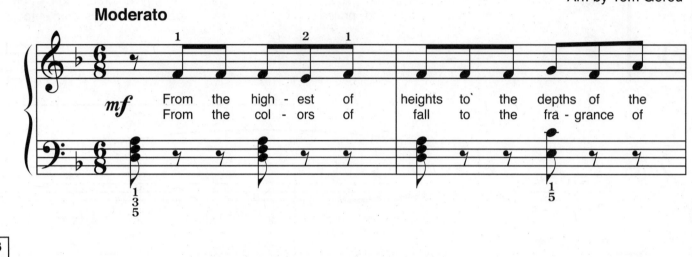

From the high - est of   heights to` the depths of the
From the col - ors of   fall to the   fra - grance of

sea,   cre - a - tion's re -
spring,   ev - 'ry crea - ture u -

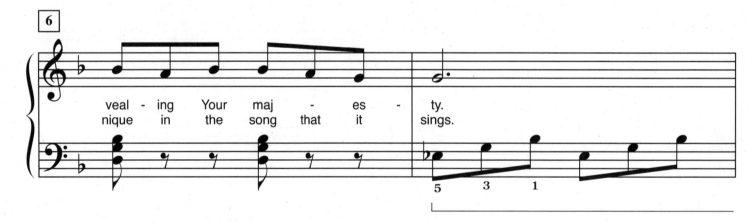

veal - ing Your maj - es - ty.
nique in the song that it sings.

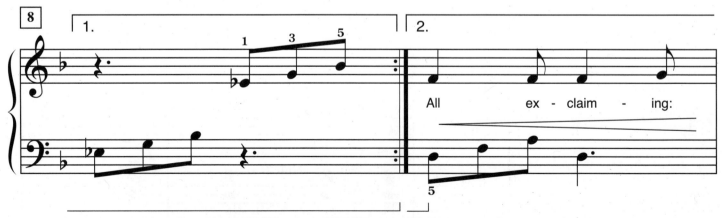

All   ex - claim - ing: